This book is dedicated to

_____

The Story of Two Girls

The 411 on me is...

Full name _____

Current address _____

_____

_____

Where I'm from _____

_____

Birthday _____

Zodiac sign _____

Hair and eye color _____

_____

Oldest, middle, youngest or only child

_____

Nicknames _____

_____

Personality traits _____

_____

_____

_____

My friend's stats...

Full name _____

Current address _____

_____

_____

Where you're from _____

_____

Birthday _____

Zodiac sign _____

Hair and eye color _____

_____

Oldest, middle, youngest or only child

_____

Nicknames _____

_____

Personality traits _____

_____

_____

_____

photo here

In the Beginning

photos of us when we first became friends

photo here

The First Day of Our Friendship

Our story began on the day of _____

We were at _____

_____

_____

I remember us meeting each other by _____

_____

_____

The first thing you said to me was _____

_____

_____

I instantly thought you were _____

_____

_____

_____

And you thought I was _____

_____

_____

_____

On that first day, my predictions of what we would become, whether friend or foe

I look back now and see how accurate my first impressions of you were. These are the things I later learned to change or confirm those impressions

From what you originally thought of me, these are the things you now believe

A detail of the day our friendship was born that I will never forget

In the Beginning

Things we did in the beginning to help our friendship grow _____

_____

_____

_____

_____

_____

_____

The one moment I knew we would become good friends _____

_____

_____

_____

_____

_____

Other friends and people who helped in establishing our friendship _____

_____

_____

Not every friendship starts out perfect. These are a few things that made ours a little rocky at first _____

_____

_____

_____

_____

_____

Destined to be good friends, little problems couldn't break us apart; here's how we solved them _____

_____

_____

_____

_____

_____

What I liked so much about you, right from the start _____

_____

_____

_____

_____

_____

What you liked about me most in the beginning _____

_____

_____

_____

_____

_____

Girlfriendship

You learn so much about a person when becoming friends. The first thing
I remember learning about you was...

One of the first things I shared with you about me was _____

_____

_____

_____

Secrets we learned to share with each other (a true sign of friendship) _____

_____

_____

_____

An interesting fact I was surprised to learn about you _____

_____

_____

_____

What I learned we had most in common _____

_____

_____

_____

_____

_____

Friends and Family

I remember the first time you met my family _____

_____

_____

_____

_____

_____

Things about me you learned from meeting them _____

_____

_____

_____

_____

I met your family when _____

_____

_____

_____

_____

I thought they were _____

✳ _____

_____

_____

_____

Special things about you your family told me _____

_____

_____

_____

_____

Your family made me feel a part of them when _____

_____

_____

_____

_____

You became a part of my family when _____

_____

_____

_____

_____

photo here

Friends are a special kind of family

photo here

Sharing = Caring

I wanted to share with you things that were important to me.

Hobbies I taught you _____

_____

_____

Activities I included you in _____

_____

_____

Events I invited you to _____

_____

_____

My favorite things that would soon become yours _____

_____

_____

Viewpoints I shared with you _____

_____

_____

_____

_____

Things that are important to you, that you wanted to share with me

Learning what's important to each other makes those things important to us. What is now important to both of us

Friendship is one of the most important things we share with one another; these are the qualities in each of us that make our friendship special

Two of a Kind

What makes us such good friends _____

_____

_____

_____

From everything we've learned from one another, this is what I like best about you

_____

_____

_____

_____

Similarities we have that keep us together _____

_____

_____

_____

_____

Our differences that keep our friendship interesting

_____

_____

_____

_____

We're together so much people say we are starting to look alike because

_____

_____

_____

What I treasure about our friendship

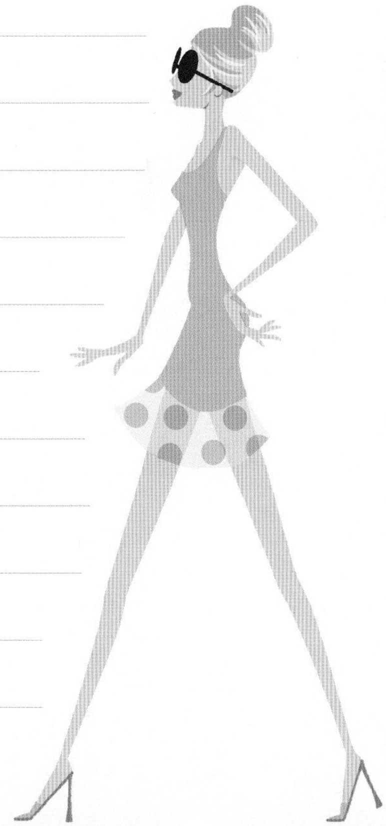

_____

_____

_____

_____

photo here

photo here

photo here

photo here

Just the Two of Us

Things we love to do, just you and I...

Most memorable time spent together thus far

_____

_____

_____

_____

_____

We could spend hours on the phone talking about

_____

_____

_____

_____

_____

photo here

photo here

photo here

photo here

These are a Few of Our Favorite Things...

Best place for "girl talk" _____

Favorite Friday night hangout _____

Movies we love to watch over and over _____

_____

Songs we sing at the top of our lungs _____

Best PMS remedy _____

"Girls only" activities _____

_____

Favorite comfort foods _____

_____

TV shows we are addicted to _____

_____

Favorite topic of gossip _____

Best place to spend the day shopping

We love to lunch at

Our drink of choice

Favorite way of staying in shape

Summertime activities

Flowers that make us smile

Best magazines to pass the time

I love to borrow from you

You love to borrow from me

Favorite way to pamper ourselves

So Not Cool

Dirty habits we dislike _____

_____

Personality traits we despise _____

_____

My biggest pet peeve _____

Your biggest pet peeve _____

People need to think before saying these things _____

_____

_____

We can't stand when other drivers _____

_____

_____

I hate to come home from a long day and _____

_____

_____

You hate to come home from a long day and _____

_____

The worst pickup line we've heard _____

Sport we would like to ban _____

Things that bug me about work/school _____

Things that bug you about work/school _____

A bad hair day is when _____

_____

Mondays are bad because _____

_____

An embarrassing moment of mine _____

_____

_____

Your most embarrassing moment _____

_____

_____

photo here

photo here

Who Is...

The most outgoing _____

The funniest _____

The dare devil _____

More conservative _____

More optimistic _____

Career driven _____

A party animal _____

Nurturing _____

The most athletic _____

More like a diva _____

Picky (when it comes to food) _____

Picky (when it comes to men) _____

The most stylish _____

More sensitive _____

More independent _____

Girl Stuff

A hundred pairs of shoes, lipstick and talking on the phone...some things never change when it comes to being a girl. The best thing about having someone to share those with...

We always love to look our best; our typical routine for getting ready to go out on the town _____

_____

_____

_____

Practically spending all of our girl time together, these silly things are bound to happen (ie: finishing each other's sentences, showing up in the same outfit, etc.) _____

_____

_____

_____

_____

_____

Girls Only

We love to feel pampered and girly. These are the things we do that most guys wouldn't dream of doing

These all-girl events are becoming tradition

An old fashioned slumber party with the girls entails

z-z-z-z-z-z-z-z-z

A car full of girls can only mean one thing...road trip! The most fun we had out on the open road

Shop till you drop! Our craziest shopping story

What's so special about not having guys around

Girls Rock

photo here

Photos of us and our
other girlfriends

photo here

photo here

photo here

Girls Rule

Along with the two of us, our extended group of girlfriends includes _____

_____

_____

_____

_____

If you could give our gang a name, it would be _____

_____

_____

_____

We cherish our other friendships because _____

_____

_____

_____

_____

People always say you learn through experience (or through your friends' experiences). Things we learn not to do from our friends

Things we learn from our other friends that make our friendship stronger

Why we think girls rule!

Such a Girl Moment

A birthday bash to remember _____

_____

_____

_____

_____

A dating disaster _____

_____

_____

_____

_____

We never laughed so hard when _____

_____

_____

_____

_____

_____

We were almost stopped by the fashion police when _____

_____

_____

_____

_____

We could blame this on PMS _____

_____

_____

_____

_____

_____

_____

_____

_____

This moment goes down in history

_____

_____

_____

_____

_____

_____

_____

_____

_____

_____

_____

_____

_____

_____

_____

_____

_____

_____

_____

photo here

photo here

Girlfriends Forever

This is How I Know Our Friendship Will Last

This is why you think we will be friends until the end

Out of all our friendships, these are things that make our friendship unique

Friends for Life

photo here

photo here

True Friends

Of course having you around for the fun stuff is fun, but it means the most when I know you are there for _____

_____

_____

_____

_____

It means a lot to me being there for you when _____

_____

_____

_____

Although it seemed impossible at the time, together we managed to get through _____

_____

_____

_____

Advice you've given me, I will always take to heart

My words of wisdom to you are

Sometimes I don't need advice, just someone to let me vent. When your shoulder meant the most

Reaching milestones in life are always meaningful, but these meant the most knowing you were there to share them with me...

A milestone of yours we celebrated together

You inspire me by

I inspire you

Over the years, you have made me a better person by

I have helped in part to make you the person you are now by

Celebrating Our Friendship

photo here

photo here

Photos of us together during the events and times that meant the most

photo here

photo here

The Good & the Bad

I didn't really understand the meaning of friendship until

You always encouraged me to do better; I succeeded at these things with you cheering me on

I cheered for you when

Even the best of friends have arguments now and then. Here are some things we have disagreed upon in the past

With a disagreement now and then, we resolve our issues by

One special thing about our friendship that makes me forget why we ever disagreed to begin with

Cheers To Our Future

What I Truly Wish for You in Years to Come...

What you wish for me

What I wish for you

...And to Our Dreams

With many dreams still to come true, I can't wait to share these things with you in the future _____

_____

_____

_____

_____

_____

_____

What you look forward to _____

_____

_____

_____

_____

_____

_____

_____

_____

_____

Goals we plan on reaching together

...and things we will never give up on

photo here

photo here

Until Tomorrow

Things we've experienced together today, which will make our tomorrows even better

_____

_____

_____

_____

_____

_____

_____

Getting older means getting wiser, not getting old. Where we see ourselves 20, 30, 40 years from now

_____

_____

_____

_____

_____

_____

_____

...Here's to Us

My toast to our friendship

Your well-wishing words to us

photo here

photo here

© 2004 Havoc Publishing
San Diego, California
U.S.A.

Text by Heidi Van Winkle

ISBN 0-7416-1962-8

Made in China